Love Letters
to GOD

Susan Sievert

NEWMAN SPRINGS PUBLISHING
320 Broad Street
Red Bank, NJ 07701

First originally published by Newman Springs Publishing 2023

ISBN 978-1-68498-982-9 (Paperback)
ISBN 978-1-68498-983-6 (Digital)

Printed in the United States of America

In honor to God, my Father, my love, Jesus, and the Holy Spirit

Refreshing Water

My soul thirsts for You
Like
The desert crying out for water
That calms its surface

And all of a sudden
The thunder breaks
The storm clouds rumble
And blessed water falls down
In drops of refreshing water—love
To refresh, renew, rekindle
Life that has been lying dormant
For the Holy One to kiss with His love
The source of power of might
The Mighty One.

Water that renews all
Things all humans
If your heart is set for life
Life of the Living God
The Living Water
Life that renews, refreshes
Fills up your cup

To the brim
With life of the heart
The soul that cries
Out for water, the
Water that only God can give

The one God hears
And answers with His love
His power, His blessings
To set you free
And fill the cup of destiny
For you are of God
He is in you
He made you in His image
The Life-Giver
The source
The source of life in body
Soul and spirit
Of all your tomorrow
And todays
For you are called to be
One with Him
Your answer defines

All your eternity
If you thirst

You are filled in the Lord Jesus
Your soul shouts out, O Lord
In the heavens
On the earth

For all to hear
Of your love
In your Father God
Jesus and the angels
Sing a new song of praise
Unto the Lord God

For He is perfect
In all things and humans
He refreshes with His
Life-giving water
For a new life, a new love
A new beginning
In the Lord Jesus

The Spirit of Your Love Shines

Smile at me, O Holy Virgin Mother
Shine the brilliance of your smile on me
Let the warmth of your beauty enfold me
Let me find comfort in your arms

When I am so alone
All I have to do is think of you
And the shadows fall away
Making darkness into day

When I lay my head on my pillow
I can feel the love of your
Embrace enter into my soul a mother's love
A strength I've never known before
You are my mother
And I can endure the pain
And can love once again
Tomorrow doesn't scare me anymore
For the strength that you give
Makes me just want to live

Every day in the sunshine
Of your smile loving you
Cloudy days are like
Sunshine days
For the spirit of your love
Enfolds me gently wherever I am

Your Love Fills My Heart

God, my Father
Being in Your loving hands
Seeing Your smile
Your perfection
Your beauty is beyond
Happiness
It is ecstasy

Knowing You love me
With all my shortcomings
Yet You care for me
It is beyond anything
I can understand
Knowing You love me
Is divine perfection in action
Pure and wondrous
Beyond compare
Bringing the thought
Of Your joy and love
To my heart
My soul is full of longing
For You
When I call, You are there
When I cry, You dry my tears

When I'm sad
You comfort me
When I am sick
You heal me

You heal my aching
Heart, body, and soul

You laugh with me
You cry with me
You dry my tears
You take pleasure
In my happiness
Like a father
Watching his child grow
To be the best person
He or she is meant to be
In love, mind, and spirit

Like a teacher You teach
By example
And love like a God
My only God

You are there
To take my hand
Especially when I fall
You pick me up and dry
My tears
Until there is joy
In my heart

Knowing You makes me
The happiest person on earth
For in Your love
I can be me

With You by my side
To guide my steps
Right into Your arms
Living where I was
Meant to rest forever
Until there is joy
In my heart even though my
Heart still aches
My spirit soars
On the wings of an eagle
I can see the highest reaches
And beyond the wonder
The perfection that is You

The Stones Cry Out to Me

The stones cry out
To give me glory and praise
When men's hearts grow cold
With indifference and hate
They shame God's very soul
And even nature cries to calm the
Very heart of God
For even nature
Cries out to me
To give me praise
For men know not what they do
Even when they know
They don't care, says God

Sad will be the day
When destiny and justice
Comes quickly knocking
At your door
Oh, men of evil ways
—And you are lost and
Your false gods
Don't respond
Where will you be, who will
You call on

Oh, evil men of cold hearts
Your time is coming
Is already here
Repent before it is too late

And the doors shut
And you are left to your will
And your chosen place
Is in the hellfire
You so love

God Is Love for You

God is great of mercy and love
God of pardon and blessings
God's tears fell
Upon His Son's pure body, the body
Of Jesus on the cross
And washed away
The most precious
Blood unto the world
To save it from itself

That's why He gave
His only Son Jesus
To die on the cross
For you
So, your life can
Be lived in heaven
For all eternity
He died on the cross
Yet He lives again
To deliver you
Out of bondage
From your problems
From your sins
That chain you to perdition

That weigh you down
And won't let you be
In Him you find

Peace and understanding
That money cannot give you

How long will your heart?
Be cold
As you turn away
From your Savior
Jesus Christ

Come to Me

God let His light shine on you
He said, "I love you no matter what
I am here for you
In the midst of your problems
You will find peace in Me
Among all your troubles
I'll be helping you along
Call Me and I will answer
I am walking next to you
Just listen to My voice
In your heart, in your soul
And My love will wash over you
I walk in your footsteps and am beside you
And listen to your dreams
I call your name
In Me you will find love
And strength to go on

"I'm happy when you are happy
I cry with you in your pain
For I made you
In My image
I fashioned you
Out of dust out of the earth

"I gave you
A soul, a heart to love
A heart to believe in me
A heart to love me

A destiny to fulfill
Different from anyone else

"I didn't say it was going
To be easy to follow Me
I am there with you
So, you are never alone
Even now
I don't hear My name—Jesus
In your voice, in your life, in your soul
I still keep hoping that
You love Me, that you will
Come to Me before
It is too late
For the night draws
Near and long
And I wait for you
In your discontent
For today may be your
Last day
Live it wisely with love"

All Praise Be to You

Praise You, praise You
Praise You, my Lord God
God of heaven and earth

Praise be to You by all
The angels in heaven
Praise and glory be to You by
All the stars in the sky
God's universe
Praise You. By all the sons
Of our Father God
That He has made
Praise You all the earth
And sky,
Heaven's beauty
Sings to You
All of nature sings to You
Praise be to You by all
The people who love You
Of every nation on earth

Praise You all the
Moons in the heavens
Glory and praise to
Our Lord Jesus Christ God

Praise be to You
Father, Son, and Holy Spirit
Voices of nature

Praises be by all
The voices of men

Joining all in jubilation
Praising our God
Of heaven and
Earth and all that you are
I praise You, Lord God
Let the whole earth
And heavens above
Praise You, Father
Son and Holy Spirit
Who is, was, and
Forever will be

A New Hope, A New Day

Father God and Holy Spirit
Jesus, I love Your springtime
Flowers budding and
Blooming everywhere
Birds singing in the air
I just love Your creation
The whole world is in
Awe of Your renewal
Of fresh spring breezes
It makes the heart feel
Fresh beginnings

Time to start over
Another year
Of promise and love

A new hope, a new love
A new song to sing
Beautiful skies
A new day, new beginning
All because of You, my God

Thank You

Thank You, Father
For listening to my call
Thank You, Father, for
Not letting me fall

For Your loving touch
I love so much
I thank You

Out of the darkness
When my soul was
In fear and pain
You came down
To dry my tears

You touched me with
Your softness
Your soothing voice, Your grace
You held me in
Your loving hands

You kissed my pain away
You held me till
The darkness fell
Into light

I can understand the way
Of Your greatness
And Your love

For when I called
Your name
You stood, by my side
And gave me peace and hope
The greatness of
Your loving touch
Gave peace to my soul
You brushed my tears away
And gave me peace and strength
That only You can give
With Your loving touch
Your love came over me
To calm my fears
And still my heart
Thank You, God my Father
Thank You, God the Son
Thank You, Holy Spirit
For in God, three
Are one
For answering my prayers
As only You can do
For out of the darkness
I found myself in Your light
Shining through

You held me in
Your Holy hands
As only You can do
In doing so
You blessed me with love
Of pain and despair to overcome
And made me new

And waking up, I find
You saved me from despair
Of illness and pain
Thank You, God Almighty
Father, Son, and Holy Spirit
All three are one
Thank You and praise
Your holy name for all the time

Thank You, God

Thank You, God my Father

Thank You for your gift
Of Your precious Son Jesus
Because of His suffering
And love of You and humanity
He came to set all pilgrims free
Free to love the only God
Who was and is and
Will always be
Thank You, God, I thank You
My heart is full of love for You

With all my being I sing
Thanksgiving and praise to
The Holy God I love

Thank You, thank You, thank You
God, I thank You and
Praise Your holy name
Who was and is and is to come

Thank You from
The bottom
Of my heart and soul
For all Your love

Thank You, for all the
Gifts and blessings
That only You can give
For Your healing touch
Your gentleness
Your blessedness
I thank You

Thank You, Jesus, God

Thank You, my Jesus
For loving me
Thank You, Jesus
For setting me free

Free from the bonds
That held me tight
Free from the evil
One's delight
Thank You
For breaking the chains
Of darkness and fear
For blessing me
With courage and strength
As I watch the arrows
That fly and seeing You
Break them in half
For my delight

No matter what comes
My way
You are there
To help me fight
My battles

For a winsome situation
For You are the great God Almighty
Where nothing and no one

Can withstand Your power
For You made the heavens
And earth and everything in it
Thank You for setting
My soul free
Thank You for every
Gift of thee
Thank You for
The refreshing drink
That is You, Jesus
Thank You for me
Thank You for my faith in You
You came to set
All prisoners free
Thank You, my God
I sing to Thee
With faith and love
I praise Thee

How great and wonderful You are
For You made the
Heavens and the earth
All the angels and
Man to worship You—always
If not, they go into
Perdition with the
Evil angels
And the people who
Don't love You or praise
Your Holy Name
For You alone are holy

You alone are the Lord
God, Father, Son, and
Holy Spirit
I praise You, I worship
You Father, Son, and Holy Spirit, I praise You

Your Love Falls over Me

God Almighty
I hear Your singing
Rejoicing over me with
Your blessings
Overcome with delight as for everyone
When You made me, the angels sang
I hear the flutter of their wings
Beautiful leaves of the trees
And the butterflies and birds singing
Your blessings of the
Streams of the mountains
In the trickle of the brook
In the fish living there
I feel Your touch, Your warm embrace
In the sunshine breeze
In the soft breezes and in
The soft breath of Your blessings
For me and everyone who wants to love You
I feel Your love flow
Over me
In the soft raindrops
As Your warm caress
When they trickle on my skin

When the sun shines
I feel Your beautiful smile
And hear Your laughter
In the mountains and valleys

As nature enjoys itself
In Your creation

You sparkle in the rainbow
And in the starlit sky

In the stillness of the night
I hear Your voice speak
To my soul
In a soft whisper
In the stillness of the night, You call
In my dreams, You come
With all Your beauty
And Your soft smile that
Envelops me
I feel
Your soft embrace
Your loving blessings
Where You touch the edge
Of reality

And I am alone with You
In my dreams
In my slumber I feel
Safe in Your hands
With Your protection
Nothing to hurt me
As You slay the dragons
With a glance to my delight
And in my wakefulness, You are there
Directing me in the path
I should go

In everything
I thank You and praise
You for being my
Father God
Of heaven and earth
And all that is

The Heavens Cry

The heavens cry
The earth is in turmoil as
The heavens cry
The heavens shake in
Great thunder and lightning
To see the pain
Of God's love rejected
The earth shakes
And the heavens roar
To see the Son of God
On the cross suffering
For you and me
While men gamble for
His garments
And greed and sin
Carries on
As if there is no tomorrow

Not a care in the world
While Jesus God suffers
For them, for us
Careless men in a
World of unbelief

But Jesus, God is not dead
He is alive
And will return
To see where you stand
In the test of time

With or without Him
No one escapes
He is the risen Christ
Make the change now
Before it is too late
And the gates of hell
Open for you
Only you can shut
Them with your love
For Jesus God
Your repentance
As you set aside your unbelief
With love
And caring for the
One who gave His life for you

Mother of Jesus

Dear Mother of the universe
We call your name in wonder

The heavens shine
With your splendor
With your heavenly grace

We call you blessed
Because you have been
The chosen one to birth the Christ Child Jesus
For all time
To see our Lord come
To life to be one with Him
For your loving hands
Helped Him and blessed Him
In all His wonder
You carried Him in your womb
Your loving heart was
The first to love Him
The new Christ Child
As the world would
Love Him not

Mother dear, your love
Covers the earth
With your love for us
Are we too blind to see,
To feel
Our hearts too cold

To love you back in return
To honor you to be so chosen
Still your love call us
Will we hear it in our hearts
Do we answer your call
Or remain silent
Pretending we don't
Hear you calling
We don't feel your love for us
For even in the lonely night
You are there
Showering us with blessings
With the Christ Child
In your arms
Loving Him, caring for Him
Ever the mother
We long for
Hearing our cries
For help
Prayers of hope
And blessings
Till you stop and turn
And see us
With our arms
Outstretched
To you and the Christ Child
The answer to our prayers
Showering us with love
How long can we go on
Not believing your words
Until too late
We find that tomorrow is now

With the door closing
The day of the Lord
Both of you still calling us
And you in your very heart
Loved us, prayed for us
To come to Jesus

But our cold hearts turned
Away because of our unbelief
Our indifference and pride
And the dark days come and
Find us all alone
Don't let it be that way for you
Let's pray to change the world
In heaven's name

Queen of Peace,
Queen of Love

O Mary
Queen of peace
Let your love never cease
To bring to us
Your message dear
That will ring
Throughout the year

That only love can
Mend a heart
That by caring can
Dispel the fear
And by loving, we
Can come close to God
And close to you, O Mary
Mother of Jesus, mother of all
Today's hurts don't move
So much
When put into the
Victor's cup
Where Christ Jesus
Takes the pain
And blesses us
In heaven's name

Beautiful Heart

Oh, beautiful heart of Jesus
Beating with a love so strong
No man can comprehend
All the gifts You are ready
To bestow on those who truly love You

You are ever ready to shine
The light of Your radiant love
Graces flowing in never-
Ending abundance
To fall on those whose
Hearts are open to You

Let our hearts be open
To Your love
And being blessed
With Your loving graces
We will return
True love to You

We will return to
Your loving arms
Never more to be unbelieving
Never more to be in question
Or lost and lonely again

I Shall Not Wonder

I shall not wonder
About heaven
Or what my gift
Shall be

The only thing
My heart desires
Is to be near to God, my
Jesus, my Lord and Savior

That gift alone
Is heaven
And everything to me

For peace and love
And angel smiles
Shall be my destiny

Queen of Heaven and Earth

My mother dear
Queen of heaven and
Earth, how can I put into words
The majestic royalty the supremeness
The beauty beyond beauty
That is you
That to my very soul
Is life
O Virgin Mother
My heart fills with
Love for you, my mother
You sit in splendor
In the storm in the heavens
The clouds dancing and swirling
Around you to do
Your every bidding

The teardrops fall
From my eyes as
I watch praying my rosary
In joyful thanksgiving
From my heart for your love
I try to put your beauty
Into words
My love into song

How can I with my
Imperfections
Describe such

Exquisite splendor
And majesty
As the queen of heaven
And earth

You sit in all
Royal calmness and
Royal splendor
As the night turns
Into day
With the electricity
Of the storm
Swirling around you

As I watch in wonder
Your sereneness
Where you make
The clouds your armchair
And footstool
With baby Jesus in your arms
How I long to rush
Into your loving presence
Into your heavenly arms
In such a storm
Of thunder and lightning
But my heart stays still
As I gaze in wonder
Of you
For you know I see you
You wish to let me know
That you are queen of heaven
And earth

The lights dance around you
In your quietude
You bring peace and
Joy to my heart
With Jesus in your arms
Your love is all enfolding
To the ends of the earth
And heaven itself rejoices
For you alone are our
Heavenly mother, queen of heaven and earth

You Choose

You accuse and you slander
You whisper in corners among yourselves
Thinking no one hears
No one cares about your fellow men
There is God who cares, who loves
Who is listening to every word
And He does not forget

You testify with intent
To hurt, you profess untruth
As if it was truths to cover
To hurt to cause pain
But the angels of God
Write every word of truths
And untruths, the sly looks and lies
Every action and inaction
Everyone has a book
That shall be opened
At judgment day
The story of your life
Before the great Judge—God
You choose what you
Want in it, good or bad
In your book

Why not make it good
You will be judged on it
We are all going
To be judged

You and I for good or bad
Let's be judged for being good
Listen, the Four Horsemen
Of the apocalypse are
Coming, are already here
Sifting the wheat
From the weeds
Do you want to be grain or a
Weed, you determine your destiny
What you are
And where you
Want to go

Jesus is here
Wanting to help you
But you decide
He will not force you to go His
Way, He will be waiting
For you and me, your God, our
Savior on judgment day

He holds judgment for the most part now
Choose who you serve
You choose who you serve
You choose your destiny
For all time
Happiness in heaven or burning suffering in hell
Time travels as it were
All roads
Smooth, crooked, and
Treacherous

Choose the road to life
To Christ Jesus who died for you
He said
"I am the truth
And the life
No one comes to the Father
Except through Me
For I am the life, the truth
The road—the word
The destination
For all time
I'm waiting on you
And for you
With open arms, choose Me, your God
Your Savior Jesus Christ"

Great Is Your Love

Great is Your love
And your mercy, O God
Wonderful and worthy are You

I worship You and give You thanks
For all of the greatness
That You are
I give You glory and praise
Mighty and merciful
Loving and kind
There is no other
God but You

You alone are worthy to behold
Worshipped and glorified
As a great and mighty God
Forever and ever
Amen
The heavens sing to Your
Glory, and the earth
Dances in joyous wonder
Of being blessed
By You
God of all

Enjoying God's Blessing

The leaves are fluttering
And dancing on the trees

Like the doves dancing
On the cedars of Lebanon

While the breeze carries
Them softly in the light of day

That's how I feel as
I sit in the sun
Enjoying God's blessings
After long and cloudy days
Wet with rain

I see the flowers sparkling
In the sunshine
As a shower of love falls on them
Rain kissed with goodness
Showers of delight
Now basking in the sun

After a long river
Of raindrops
Kissing as it were their beautiful
Faces saying I love it

Stay with me awhile
For I bring you life

Diamonds in the Sun

Snow in the sunshine
The sun is shining
After beautiful falling snow
I see the snowflakes as it were
Through the sunrays
Falling in a special place God
Has ordained for them as if saying
"Come and play with me awhile
As I make You sparkle
Like diamonds in the sun"

Watching God's wonders
Materialize before my eyes
Visual masterpieces
Of perfection
Falling softly, softly
On my skin
The kiss of nature
And God, my Creator

Sprinkling snow
Through the sunlight
Before everything
Turns white

How many snowflakes
Does it take
To make a snowball
Cover a hill

Blanket a mountain
Only God knows

And I sit here pondering
At the excellence of
God's magic touch
The wonders He performs

God's great works of art
His masterpieces
Ever changing
His excellence
In all He does
In great love and abundance
Perfection in all His works

Every day a beautiful
Glorious day, a beautiful day
In God's creation

Heavenly Songs

Jesus, Jesus, Jesus
Your name resounds in the heavens
The sun, the moon, the stars
Sing to your glory
Day and night without ceasing
They sing and praise
The Son of God and Father God
Glory to You, Lord

Holy God and Father
The angels praise You
All day long
The stars take up the
Song in evening tide
To praise You with
Colors beyond the
Rainbow with words
No man has ever heard

The heavens have their
Music all their own
With patterns in the sky
And creations in
The stars
No man has ever seen
Music so heavenly
Only You know
For they sing to
You, Lord God Almighty

Son and Holy Spirit
The great I AM
Who created the
Heavens and the earth
For His greater glory

Created men to glorify
Him, women and children
And all of nature
For His greater glory

Sing, oh, earth
A new song
For God has
Smiled upon you

Shining My Love on You

As light flurries
Are falling
Twinkling like jewels
In the crispness
Of the morning
Light snow flurries shining
Through the clouds

Millions of sparkles
Are falling
Down from the sky
Like angels in the vastness
Of God's heavenly place
Flying, filling the
Expanses of heaven, ever
Fulfilling God's intended will
To shine on all humanity
With His nurturing blessedness

Sleep Blessings

The sun envelops me
So warm
With loving arms
And tender rays
Of soft embrace
It sets me all aglow

I feel so warm and nurtured
As in a cocoon—a womb
Where I get my warm
Nourishment
That fills my body in bliss
In warm feelings
That all is well
If only for a while

And I fall into my world
Of sleep
I surrender to the warmth
And contentment floating as it were
In a world of slumber
As my spirit and body
Soar into the light

And I am nurtured
By the sun
In the warm embrace
Of sleep
As I lay in contentment

I slumber
To be refreshed
For a new day
That is coming
With all its promises

Beautiful Delight

God, as You spoke to me today
With Your beautiful
Perfect jewels
Flowers so beautiful
Only You could have painted
A flower such as a columbine
Perfection shining in its beauty
Light purple tipped with yellow
Long graceful tips
Yellow center
Petals opening its face
To the sun and sky
Reaching up to
Touch the soft summer light
As if to say, "Thank You, God" for me, for us
Her beautiful face
A face of soft wonderful colors
If it could talk
I know it would praise You
Which it does just being itself

How much more is Your caring
Love for us, O God
A love so splendid
Warm and wonderful

Never failing to bring
Warmth and love
Of many splendid moments

Of time
That stands still
Yet travels in the
Expanse of time
To be made perfect
In You.

Praise and Glory

Praise be to God
My loving God
My wonderful God
My beautiful and
Merciful God
My uplifting God
My powerful God
My creating God
I praise You, I worship You
Praise and glory be to You
My saving Father God
My uplifting God
Praise and Glory
Be to You, my glorious God
Oh, most gracious God
Giver of life
With treasures of love—and gifts too numerous to count
Thank You, Father God, the Great I am
My miracle God
My creative God
Praise be to You
Who was and is
Who will be
Forever and evermore

A God who is
The beginning, the end
Who is there for you always
Praise and glory

Be to You, Most High God
My everlasting Father God
My glorious God
Praise and worship
And glory
Be to You
Most High God
Your love surpasses
All understanding
My precious God
We are blessed
Beyond all measure
Because of You
Almighty God and Father

The Beauty That Is You

Holy Virgin Mary
Contemplating on your beauty
Blessed Virgin Mary
Knowing that all the jewels
Surrounding you
Lose their splendor
Their brilliance in comparison
To your beautiful countenance
O Holy Mother of God
Mother of all people
The whole of heaven
Calls you blessed
Blessed to be
The mother of God—Jesus
God's only Son

All nature and all of heaven
Marvel and sing to you
O Holy Virgin Mary, Mother of all
Every flower in bloom
Brings to mind
The beauty of your smile

Knowing that
Nothing on earth
Can compare to the
Beautiful vision of you
And no feeling
Can compare

To your enfolding
Love for us
O Virgin Mary, our
Mother
For in you we find contentment
Joy, love, peace, and
Gentleness that no one
On earth can give or provide
O blessed mother of
The Christ Child
We honor you and bless you
Thank you for your
Love and goodness

The Great Power of God

The power of His voice
Shook the heavens into being
He let out His breath
And the sun appeared
Smiling in all His glory
And splendor
And the winds came into being with His love
The earth shook
The rivers answered
In their rush to the sea
In joy and happiness of their creation
The mountains laughed
With breezes running
Skipping through the trees

At the happiness of the
Earth becoming a
Beautiful place
For all that is to be and
All of humanity

And the flowers
In joyous wonder
The great power of God
Of a God who created them
Swayed and winked at the sun
When all the while
The lovely bees
Nestled in their

Petals giving sweetness
To their strength

And God looked and
Saw it was good
His creation coming
Into being

For tomorrow would
Be a new beginning
As today
And the heavens
Trembled with delight

And the stars
Added their brilliance
To this new day full of promise
The twinkling and sparkle
In God's eyes, they rejoiced of
Coming into being
For great were the days
The delight of God

The clouds danced and swayed
In the breeze
Running to and fro
And the earth took
Shape with all its blessings
And God called it good

And God smiled on His creation
And the earth sang
In all its glory
To the one who made them
And the heavens answered
Amen, amen, and amen

To God Give the Glory

To God my Father
Who is everything
To all those who
Believe in Him

To everyone
Even if they don't
Know Him yet
May He speak
To your heart and soul
And make all things
New to you
In your heart mind
And spirit
Body and soul
In this life and the next

To God give the glory
Forever and ever
From your heart and soul
And the heavens said
Amen, amen, glory to God
For all that He is
And continues to be

The Wonderful Power of God

I marvel at Your perfection
God my Father
That You have made
The world
And all that is in it
Is such a short time
And in such perfection

You who made the
Human body
With all its complexities

The humming bird in its
Great beauty and strength
The butterfly that travels
Far and beyond on high mountaintops
The beautiful sky
The singing sun
With its warming rays
All for me

You made
The snow-topped mountains
The flurries
In the wind
The thunderous waters
The waterfalls

Mighty as can be
You made the sparkling
Brook with life-giving
And tasty fish
You made the sand so soft
That tickles my toes
When I walk
That make the footprints
In the sands of time Yours and mine
You made the rocks
Of granite and stone
The wonderful jewels
Of color
In all perfection
The honor is all Yours
My God and Father

The honor is Yours
All Yours
The wonderful power of God
I marvel at the whispering winds
The snowflakes in their diversity

The falling leaves, all their colors and shapes
Your gentle touch of
Rustling breezes
The clouds as white
As snow
Where I dream of
Playing and flying
To and fro
And of a nap on a

Soft caress of Your love
So tender perfection in all its glory
The flowers of many colors
The stones of every hue
And strength
The honor and glory are Yours
The woman and man
The love therein You made
So much like You in their creation
In all Your wonder
A wonder so true, never an end
And full of Your glorious
Power and love
How wonderful
Is Your love, Your beauty
And Your perfection
My great God and Father

The Love of Creation

In the beginning when time stood still
When the void was deep and quiet
There was a voice of quiet stillness and calm
Ringing out in the great beyond
And the void took notice
Of this new beginning
And the great voice said
"Let there be light"
And darkness fled away
To be called night

And when God said
"Let there be light"
The dancing light
Took form in the
Sun of suns
And smiled across
The emptiness
To warm the darkest places

And when it came to men
He warmed the dirt clay and
Fashioned him
Into the beautiful
Man named Adam
And loneliness
Laid him to sleep
And when he awoke

There stood Eve
In all her glory

Loneliness fled
And happiness walked in
To the heart that God had
Made in Adam, the first
Man, and so was the love of God
Manifested in creation

Where Is Your Love for Me?

Did I hear you say
There is no God
A child of God
Who does not know God, his Creator
Who is the answer
To his questions
To his prayer
Who feels his aching
Heart cry out
Unbelieving yet
Wanting to believe

God still loves you
Even though you say
He is not there
In your private times
He hears you cry
He knows your pain
Your sorrow
Your happy days
And all your tomorrows

Jesus died for all
Those who
Believe and disbelieve
When men's heart
Would not pray with Him and for Him
When tears fell
Like raindrops

With His heart broken
And all alone on the cross
The crown of thorns piercing His brain
When the nails found
His flesh
And the spear pierced
His side and blood drops raining down His body
He did it for us
He had us in mind
Even with our unbelief
Calling your name
And mine

Seeing Him suffer
Does it touch your heart
Do you feel the pain
"I suffer for you," He said
"I long to hear you say
You love Me"

Where is your love
That you try to rip
My heart to shreds
Oh, man of stone, cold as ice
Your unbelief pierces
My heart
As you strike My body
And hurt My soul
For I live forever
Because I am
Your God, your
Savior Jesus Christ

Come and believe in Me
Like the thief on the cross
I will change your
Hate into love
And save your soul
From the fires of hell
Into paradise
You can do it if you
Choose Me for your God

Jesus's Perfect Love

When the crown of thorns
Pierced His brain
Did you feel His pain
Pierce your heart
The crown of thorns like nails
When His blood ran down
In rivers of fiery pain
Crying out your name
"Where are you, do you love Me
You still don't believe in Me
Do you care
I still believe in you"
He said
"Your name is written
In My heart of hearts
And this I do for you

"Knowing someday soon
You will tell Me
You love Me
And believe in Me too
Believe in Me
My son, my daughter"
He calls you out
Saying He was and is
And am already here

Saying I believe in you
Even now as time

Has stood still
In the heavens
Knowing His pain
And sacrifices
The heavens cry—do you cry
And God Himself
Cries out in pain
He knows what is to be
Man, where is your love
For the one who has given
His life for you

If even then your
Heart is cold
The moon will cry
The sun hides his face
In sorrow over
Your unbelieving heart
For the elements know who made them
And the stones and mountains
Rivers and streams
Birds and beasts
The whole of earth
And heaven know
The stars and the whole universe
Will praise and give glory
To My name, Jesus, the Son of God
For even they know
I am their
Living God Creator
Oh, man of unbelief
The day will come

When you will cry tears
Of pain and remorse
When I rise to heaven
Yet I will love you
And come to help you
If you only ask
Cry out to Me your
Savior, and I will
Turn night into day
Pain into joy
Hate into love
And you will praise
Me your Savior, your God

Come to Me to Life

And you thought I was
Just a man called Jesus
With your heart disbelieving
Cold as stone, you reject Me
I am your Savior, your Redeemer
How you trample on
My love for you
My heart that cares for you
Yet I forgive you
Hoping you will
Turn to Me
Like the thief on
The cross and say
"Remember me
Think of me on Your way to heaven"
But you have to
Believe in Me
And try to see beyond your pride
Past your pain, your unbelief

As My tears fall
And My blood blesses you
Every day to life
Come to Me
It's not too late
Unless you make it so
It's not too late
For Me to love you, for I love you already
To forgive you

Believe in Me
Your Lord and Savior
God Jesus Christ
And your pain will be
Sweet as wine
And fly away
In My presence
Your Lord and
Savior Jesus Christ
When you are with Me
And for Me
I am your best friend
And Savior
In Me and with Me
You will never die
But have everlasting life
Your soul will live in Me forever

Jesus, I Love Your Blessings

Jesus, You bring
Sunshine into our world
And make the dark days light
As masterpieces of delight to my soul
The seasons are Your blessing
Your sunshine and abundance
In the spring, the raindrops fall
The flower spring up to
Kiss the sun a new hello
The birds cry out their song
In thanksgiving to God
With a blessing to all
With their brilliance
And happy faces and hearts

The earth renews itself
For another season
Another year

Summer, Your true abundance
Of golden fields of grain
Of fruit and harvests
For another year, another time

Songs of Wonder

God, when You created the angels
They burst forth
In song to You
Their loving God

They collected
The rays of sunshine
The dewdrops
On the grasses
And made a glittering halo
Of love and adoration
To the one who gave
Them life

They wrote their love
In heaven
Made of clouds and
Rainbows shining bright
Ever-changing panoramic
Visions of love to You

They collected the music
Of the streams and rivers
And waterdrops
The breezes took
Them up to heaven
And wrote a poetry
And dance of nature
All of which You

Had created, my God
They worshipped You
In glorious songs
And praises
They praise You all
Day long in endless
Songs of gratitude and praise
All day long into the night
With endless glitter
Of stars dancing
To Your music
For Your glory

And the perfect voices
Filled the heavens
With all of nature's
Notes of creation

Songs of wonder
In praises to their
Creator God of all ages
Who lives forever and ever
For all eternity
One and only God
Our Father

The sound of music
Was born to the sound
Of raindrops beating in refrain
Of rolling thunder
Rushing waters and tide
Caressing the seashore

In their rush to please
And trickling brooks of fresh sparkling water
And saying we are joining the great creation of
God

Love Letters to God

Love letters to God
Flown on the wings
Of a dove
Written on a paper plane
Sent them flowing, flying
Off to God
And hearing and seeing
He reaches down
And collects them
In His beautiful and
Marvelous hands, wonderful
Beautiful and loving
He reads every word
You wrote in your heart and mind
Of hearts to Him
And says
That's My loving child
That I love

Jesus, Your Name Is Love

Jesus, Your name is like
Sparkling streams of love
That runs into a
Flowing river of
Love, strength, and emotion
It brings to mind all that You are and can do
You name is soft and
Gentle music to my ears
And joy to my heart and soul

Jesus, Your name is poetry in endless love
When I say Your name
I hear music and laughter
All rolled into one

The most beautiful name
Ever spoken
The softest music to my soul
Ribbons of flowing emotion
Strength and compassion
Ring out in my soul
Salve to my heart
To my hurts

As you ease the pain
And Your love
Comes shining through
I love You
With all my heart

And soul
Glory and praise to You
And thank You
For all that You are
Thank You for
All Your blessings
That fall like
Raindrops on me
I thank You.

Jesus, My Love

The name of Jesus brings
Streams of flowing water
Pouring forth
That quenches the thirst of my soul

Jesus Christ, the most beautiful
Name in all the world
Perfect in every way
Today, yesterday, and tomorrow
Praise to our Lord Jesus Christ
The sweetest, softest loving
Sound in all the world
No other name to our
God-man named Jesus
No other name
Compares to Yours

Shower Blessings

God says, "Come
Let Me shower you
With love and protection
While I cause the heavens
To shine on you
With My blessings
In My creation
While I make your enemies
Your footstool"

Of Wisdom

I looked upon wisdom
And she did not want
To be dressed in robes
Of gold and silver

She already possessed
These things
She sparkled of beauty
Of love, of knowledge

Robes of finery were
For pretentious men

Instead she chose to be
Dressed in purity of white
Clean and beautiful as
For her betrothed
For in her is purity
Of soul, of truth, and complete love

She is worth more than
Silver and gold
Diamonds and rubies
All precious stones
Dim in her beauty and brilliance

For to have her is to possess
Beauty beyond compare
Knowledge beyond knowledge

Riches beyond riches
To know her is to love her
When you find her

She is the treasure of treasures
The greatest of treasures
The greatest and richest
Treasure there is

She causes you to do
The right thing
To go the right way
To be the best that you can be
She travels the road
With you to be a witness
To your fellow men

In her the light shines in
The darkness and the
Dark cannot penetrate
Her brilliance

The sheer beauty of her
Dressed in clouds of
Purity and goodness
Takes your breath away

She is there for the asking
She wishes to be part
Of you if only
You invite her in
And when you do

Call her
Truly want her

She comes in all her
Magnificent and simplicity
Dressed in her beautiful truth
With radiance and joy to behold

She is there for you
To encourage you
To love you
To be a part of you
And help you be
The great human being
You were meant to be

In her is all happiness
Her treasures
Never ending
She loves you and wants
To be part of you
If you only truly want her
In your heart and soul

Say yes to her
She is a great value for you
On your journey through life
She waits on you

God, Can You Hear Me?
Then Heal My Pain
with Your Love

God, I don't want my heart
Full of pain
To hurt You again and again
By not showing that I love You
As I walk my walk on life's road

I want to know You to feel
Your love to embrace You
In every step of my life
You promised the desires
Of my heart, and I take
That literally

I am full of pain
Because I don't feel
Your love
I need for You to come
Into my heart and
Stay forever

To heal the pain
To make me feel again
I am tired of feeling angry
Disillusioned
Questioning and in despair
I long for You

I'm tired of feeling bland
And not seeing
All the love You seem to
Give to someone else

Where am I in the scheme
Of things
Do I matter
Open my eyes to see
And remove the blindness
In my heart and soul

Do I count, do You hear me
Do You feel the pain
In my soul
Do You hear me calling out
To You in desperation and pain

If You do, then answer me
Heal me, make me live again
In the goodness of Your heart
In Your loving touch
In Your sweet embrace
Is where I want to be

When I cry out in tears
Alone in the pain of my heart
I need You to love me
With all Your heart
Come and heal this person that I am
To be one with You
Heal the negativity others have put on me

Doing that for me
Turns night into day over
Darkness into light
That's what I feel in my heart

Open the door
And let the sun shine in
Let the clouds fade away
And take my unbelief
And replace it with
Your abiding love

So that no more
Will I say or think
I don't believe You
I don't love You
Because at the bottom
Of my very soul
My love, my pain is crying
Out to You
Hear me, heal me
Be patient with me
Because You are perfect
And I imperfect
In the scheme of things
You are the only one
That matters
Help me to know who You are
Make me whole
In Your abiding love
In the promise You have made
To be with me
Till the end of time

Your Love Is My Strength

Your love was there
When nothing else was
Thank You, God

When the sky was dark
And the sun hid away
My heart broke
In my discontent
You were there
In my sadness and sorrow
And disbelief
Your love was
Shining bright

A glimmer of Your light
I did see
Did you call me
Did I hear my name

On the wings of a breeze
Did the leaves flutter
And say hello
Even nature calls me
Because it is part of You
My great God and Father

And yes, You called my name
With arms open wide
And your smile of sunshine

Warmed my heart and soul
And I could laugh
And cry and be brave again

And life was warm
And inviting in Your love
In Your strength and still is
Your strength and courage filled
My heart and soul
To be one with You

God, You Are Wonderful

O God
The wonder of Your beauty
The wonder of Your vast
Expanse of open country
Open fields and meadows
The wonder of Your great
Extravagance of perfection
The mountains dusted with snow
The coolness of fresh air
The love I feel in my heart
How I love You for
All Your wondrous gifts
Most especially Your love
The beauty of Your great
Sun with light-giving rays
God, how I love You
God Almighty, I sing
To Your magnificence, Your perfection
Thank You for all Your gifts
For all Your wonders
Thank You for all that You are
The Spirit of life that is You
You are generous, You are beautiful
I thank You, God
The Great I am that I am

The Chosen One

God was preparing
For the chosen one
Who would save the world
And rescue men
Prepared it perfectly
For all humanity
And the heavens trembled
At such perfection of love
For mankind, the earth has not forgotten
That eventful day

Where the Son of all
God's glory—Jesus
Blessed the earth
With His presence
And the heavens trembled
At His presence
At His perfection in
Life's abundance
Jesus, His cross of life
Buried in men's souls
Looking for a light
In their indifference
In their unbelief
And finding a spark
Lit it for all men to see
What God can do in
A life freely given

To be transformed
As a light to others
Who don't believe

The Earth Has Not Forgotten

The earth has not forgotten
Where the sacred feet
Of Jesus walked

Holding close to its breast
The joy of love so close
So deep so wonderful
When through the winds
Of centuries flew the sands
And dust away when the earth was new
The earth has not forgotten
That wonderful day
Where the son of all
God's glory kissed the earth
Blessed the earth
With His own Son Jesus

And if still men remember
To give homage to the
Christ born King
All creation shall remember
The blessed one
Were it true the sons of men
Created highest of all creation
Remember the greatest gift
Of all—Jesus the Savior
Of the world of mankind
How the angels sang and rejoiced at God's perfection
For the earth has not forgotten

Shouldn't men remember too
And hold close to
Its breast perfect love
Imprinted in its heart
The love of Jesus Christ

For we know what we do
What we say

And time holds
All memories
Great and small

To follow the
Sons of men
Unto judgment

To set him free
Or to be imprisoned
In his own world
Of unbelief

The earth has not forgotten
Where the sacred feet
Of Jesus walked
To save men from himself
Have you forgotten

You Walked the Steps for Me

Holy Jesus, Holy God
Change our lives and save us
Holy Jesus, blessed one
Of the Father's only Son
Who was chosen holy Lamb
To be the sacrifice for everyone

On the cross on Calvary
You suffered hate and misery
To save us as You had done
Throughout Your life
"Love everyone" was Your advice
To follow in Your footsteps
Right to heaven's door
Where the pure in heaven's
Heart open up the door

You walked the steps
We refused to take
You bore the pain
And the disgrace

Only a love so pure
So true
Could urge You on
To do what You set out to do

You did our time on Calvary
You paid the price

And set us free
On the road of sorrows
And pain for us

After all You've said and done
Still mankind carries on
Disbelieving Your divinity
Refusing Your love
Until judgment comes
And we are left on the outside looking in
When crucified on the cross
The heavens trembled
The sun hid its light
The heavens cried
To see the shame that
Men had done to
The blessed one God's
Only perfect loving Son
But He died willingly for you and me

Heaven wept
With great distress
To see You rejected
At Your death
By the ones
You still love
You carry their, cross their pain
And God's heart
Broken by such a sight
With tears falling down
The rains could
Not hold back the pain

And washed it all away
Upon the world
The tears of God
For a new day coming
The risen Son of God

In all His glory
Triumphant and victorious
The risen Son of God

Who died to set men free
All for you and me

To save us from destruction
As you go on your merry way
Not looking right or left
As you go into the
Darkest night of your soul
In hell's hot fires

Where you will cry
For a drop of water
But the cup is empty
And looking in, you see
The holes in the bottom
And your souls cry
For water, but your sin prevails
In the hot fires
That burn forever

Repent now
Before it is too late

Where not even
I Jesus can change
The decisions
You made and lived
And so there you are
Repent now before it is too late

Your Garden of Delight

Oh, to walk in Your garden
Full of flowers full of joy

White, yellows, pink, red, and blues
The colors of the rainbow
At Your feet
The sun shining overhead
Is pure delight

The songs of the lively birds
Breaking the stillness
Of the morning

The sun shining through
The trees
Making prisms of light
Of lively colors in the stirring breeze

No place is closer
To heaven
But in a garden
Around God's feet

The cherry blossom petals
Softly falling
On their way to their
Home on the ground
To fill their destiny
Laying a carpet of color

And perfume to
Fill your heart with delight

And perfume Your feet
To soften Your footsteps
Lord
Straining at the seams
For perfection to delight You, God
The outcome of God's
Own love for you

A chosen place, a perfect place
To languish in a garden
Full of beauty
Close to nature
Close to God

My Question

For out of the blue
The arrows come
To cause you pain and sorrow
Discomfort and death
Before our time
Why is this happening

Set out to destroy
Our peace
Set it to question our beliefs our lives
As we travel through on life's roads
Or does it just happen in time

When our hearts
Were young
We did not think
Of such things

That men would be
So mean and cruel
To destroy one another
To sell their souls
To the highest bidder
We didn't think of it then being young
For acceptance
For fame
For a piece of silver
Or gold
Where is your heart

Where is your soul
Oh, men of unbelief

For you were
Not created to hate
To hurt with your words
To destroy
To slander, to accuse with untruths
To your heart's content

Change is in the air
Will you change
Or will you go
Head on to evil
Destinations

Never more
To be heard of
But to be sifted
By the hands of time

To be cast into
The lake of fire
For all eternity

Simply because
You knew more
You could do it all—not God

Look what it got you
Look where you are at
You dealt all your cards

And lost
My soul cries
For you

Turn around
Before it is too late
For yesterday is now
And tomorrow may
Not come

Praise the Lord, Oh My Soul

Praise the Lord
Oh my soul
In words, song, deeds
And action
In love to
Your fellow men

Praise the Lord
All day long in love
And join with Mother Nature
With all its beauty
Proclaiming
The existence of
God to all

Join in praising
God in song and praise
For worthy, generous, and
Wonderful is He
In all His glory
He is wonderful in all His
Ways, great and loving
Merciful and fruitful
In His blessings to His fellow men
And all His children
Full of blessings
To all His intended
He is great and faithful
In all His works

In beauty in abundance
In finery of soul and heart
For all His creation

If Mother Nature
In all God's works
Can praise Him

Why not you
Who was made
In His image

Oh, son of man
Where is your true love
For your true God

Be with Me, Lord

Jesus God, hear my plea
Let Your love come to me
Heal my heart and my soul
For I feel I've lost control

Let Your love envelop me
Please don't cast me out to sea
Even though I've been away
Jesus God, give me strength
To face the day

With Your love surrounding me
I can climb the highest mountain
I can cross the roughest sea
With You at my side

I don't want to face the dawn
Unless I have You to learn on
Open up Your arms to me
And let me feel the comfort
Of your love and protection

Let me finally see
All the tears You shed for me
In the bleakest of the night
You stood alone
To fight the fight
You alone did this for me
On the way to Calvary

When I feel so all alone
In the darkest of the night
In the shadows and fears
Of the night—of my soul
I call on You to love me
That no human being can fill
My heart, my soul, with love like You do

Let me see the shining light
Of Your love for me tonight
And help me overcome
The shadows in my soul
That threaten me

I want to see the light to feel safe
And feel Your love for me and protection
Overshadowing my days and nights
I want to be Your friend
In Your solitude
And hold You close
Return to me, O my Lord
Please don't turn away
For the days and nights are
Long and lonely
I need Your light

To see me through
The days of my life
Jesus God, I can't
Face the day and night
Without You by
My side—always

I Love You, God

Father
God, when I see Your rainbows
And see the mountains
And Your beautiful skies
I stand in awe of Your creation
Of your greatness
Of power and brilliance
And yet You worry
About me
Small in the scheme of things
But in Your eyes great
In the person You have made
In the likeness of You

And I stand and wonder
You counted the snowflakes
And made them individual

You put the sun in the sky
And put a song in my heart for You
You made the heavens
In all their glory
And Yet you care for
A bird that falls
You care
For Your children who fail You
Yet You still care for their needs
You are there for whoever
Calls on You

You listen intently
For You do not want
To miss a call
For Your help
For Your love
And not answer

You are the ever-living
God who cares for all
Perfect in all ways
The one who will answer
When no one else will

You have provided for the
Smallest creatures
Provided for all humanity
In big and small things

You are the great provider
Our loving God and Father
The great I Am
I love You, God my Father

God, I Thank You for All that You Are

God, I thank You
For Your goodness
For Your love and
Your understanding

I thank You, Lord
For Your mercy and
Intercession in my life
For all Your blessings

Lord, I thank You for
These and all Your gifts
Of love and beauty
Your heavenly wonders
That bring joy to my heart

Lord, I thank You for
Your blessings in
Each and every day
And the nights full
Of heavenly, wondrous lights
You have bestowed
Upon me and all the world
Your heavens of great beauty
I thank You for the joy
In my heart and soul
That carries me on

To victory in spite of my
Problems and shortcomings

Lord, I thank You
For the songs in my heart
And the treasures
Of your love for me

Lord, I thank You and praise You
For Your gifts of joy
And goodness of songs
In my heart and soul
And all the beauty
And love and gentleness
That is You

I thank You for
The rainbow
Of many colors
The blessings
Of Your promise

I thank and praise You for
The beauty of Your
Smile that makes me smile when I think of You
When the sun sets
Creating a panoramic
View of Your promises

I thank You for the
Thunderclouds
That cry out

Their love for You
With life-giving rain
Only You can provide

I thank You for
All that You are and do
And made for us
I thank You, thank You
And I praise Your holy name
God, my Father—our Father

Beautiful and Great Are You

O God, beautiful and great are You
I thank You for Your
Beautiful and great days
For the peace and tranquility
In my soul

Even in these troubled
Times of war and strife
I feel the splendor
That is You, Your help
Your blessings

I love the gentle sunshine
That warms my heart and soul
I can feel You near me
Gently guiding me
And nudging me
In the way that I should go

I can feel your peace
Your love in these times
And yet there is discourse
And problems all around
In my life and others
But through it all
I come out praising
You, my God
For You are the essence
Of my being

My heart sings to You
To Your excellence

You have given me
The strength to carry on
In a world full
Of temptations and evil

And yes, I thank You, God
For all Your beautiful days
For loving everyone
For your gentle touch
In our despair, Your love, Your caring
For I have felt Your
Greatness in my soul

I cannot refuse Your love
So I just praise You
In the middle of my problems
My heart cries out
With praise and love
To Your glory and strength
In a wonderful and
Beautiful song to You
My only God
My precious God and Father
May my poetry fill Your heart with love
You are my strength, my warrior
My deliverer
I am safe in Your hands
As You carry me at
The speed of sound

To Your home, Your love
Your heart
To experience Your joy
Your love, Your excellence
That is You

You Play the Strings of My Heart

Lord, You play the
Strings of my heart
You know the notes
That bring me joy

That brings a smile
That brings a song to my heart
That brings love and fulfillment
That calms the seas
The feel of panic
The sound of sorrow
The feel of pain
You calm my heart
You bore it all for me
You calm the fears
In my heart
And set me free

Lord, You play the
Strings of my heart
To perfection

You bestow the
Beauty of Your touch
You know how to
Bring life to my soul
My heart

You set the beating
Of my heart to beat
For your pleasure
You know the sunshine
Of Your smile
That sets me free
The touch of Your hand
Dispels the gloom
And in its place
Adds the glow of love
The radiance of Your love
Lights up my life
And brings me peace
Lord, I love the way
You play the strings
Of my heart

Stones: Mountains of Colors

Rocks of stone
Mountains and hills of colors
Big and beautiful
Dressed in colors of beauty
Reds and browns, white
Creamy yellows
And in between
As if in flowing motion
Yet sitting in stillness
Giving joy to its Maker
And to the world
That sees Your beauty
In stillness lay yet speaking volumes
Of Your strength
From whence You came
As a gift for all to see
And enjoy Your beauty
In ribbons of color
And in so being
You proclaim the
Wonder that is God
You, my God

How I enjoy seeing
Your beautiful colors
As if in ribbons of candy
Tempting the senses
With Your beauty

You stand still and
Beautiful as if in motion
On Your way of being
In ribbons of color
So intense and moving
Yet creating a calmness
Of flowing motion

I love to see and enjoy
A masterpiece so intense
So arresting
It stirs the soul
To delight to marvel and
To enjoy
In God's creation
And perfection
In being

Your Caring Love

When I looked upon
The sky of blue
I saw Your face
Of flowing grace

Shining upon the world
With a love of sheer delight
Of all that You had made
And blessed
To prosper the earth
With love

You did care for everyone
And everything
And You loved it
For its perfection
And delight of all creation

When You looked
Upon the world
Upon the greatness
That is You
In Your creation

You marveled at the
Joy of humanity
In its home
You made to be
Praised by it

By all
For You are God
The Creator
Praise and glory to You, God

Beautiful Pine
Dressed in White

Softly falling snow
Settling softly on the pine
Dressing it for winter show
In mounds of foamy white

On this winter morning
The pine tree sings with delight
Reaching out its arms
As if it's on parade

Showing its beauty
Gleaming in the sun with frozen icicles
Hanging on the limb tips for all to see
To feel, to touch, to enjoy
On this cold, snowy, winter day

Rising to meet its destiny
Of praising God
In all its glory
And giving beauty to the earth
Basking in the sun
With its coat of white
Twinkling in the cold
Winter day

As the snow goes
On its own merry way
To kiss others with delight

I Worship You, Lord

God, my Father
I worship You, I love You
I praise You
I give You thanks
For all Your goodness
Your beauty, Your love
Your greatness in being our God
When I look upon
The world, the works of Your hands
The heavens above
And Your beautiful creatures
My heart fills with joy
At seeing Your excellence
In creation

I love to see the stars
In the sky
Twinkling as if saying hello
Individual and yet intricate
Each in its own world
Being part of all the cosmos
For they are gifts to mankind
From Your excellence
Of being of creation
There are not enough words
To describe the love
The strength, the energy
That is You
My great God and Father

Love Shines in You, My God

God, thank You
For Your excellence
In being our God

For Your love fills my life
You are life
In all its glory

You created life
To live to shine
In the world
And everywhere
And in the utmost
Darkness of earth, You are there

In His presence
There is life
To exist in different forms
"And yet there is you, My people
My creation
I care for
Most of all," says God

Our Great God Creator

Lord God my Father, how wonderful
You are
Your gifts You have created for us
Outshine anything the world offers
The heavens sing of Your love
Your beauty, Your blessings
Of your excellence of being

The cosmos hum and sing
Of your creations, Your perfection

You made them individual
And intricate each in its own
World yet being part of
All the cosmos

How great and wonderful
You are
You are superlative
Generous and perfect in
All created persons and things

All light dims in Your presence
There is only You all-creative
All being all love
You are the only light there is
For in You, all life, all
Creativeness dims in
Your presence

Without You, nothing exists
Everything You have made
Exists to proclaim Your greatness

Your gifts to mankind
For Your gifts come
From Your excellence
In being in Your generous Spirit
In Your love and blessings
There are not enough words
To describe Your creativeness
Your strength, Your love
Your forgiveness, Your goodness
Your blessings in all Your gifts
For You are everything that
Is that was or ever will be
My Lord God and Savior
All Your beautiful works shine
In Your creation that speaks
Volumes of who You are

You are worthy to be
Glorified, worshipped, and loved
For all time into eternity

The Creativeness of God

Creator God
The heavens shine for You
To give You praise and glory
You oversee all Your works
Of your precious love

In Your presence
All light dims
For You are the Creator
The light itself
Shining on the earth
And heavens above
The light shines
In the darkness
And darkness cannot
Overcome it or fathom it
For You made it
Allowed it to be in existence

Your excellence at being
Your completeness
Overshadows everything
Above all
You are superlative above all
For everything exists
Because of You and for You
Your light giving rays of love
Shine

Where no one
Has seen Your perfection
In time yet it exists by love
That infuses all life
Of exactness and completeness

You are the only light
I see my Creator God
For You are perfect
In all ways
There is no one to
Compare to You
No, not anyone

I Am Your Only God
That Loves You

Did you say there is no God
You who have been
Created in My image
I care for you
I decree My supremeness
Says God
No gods of stone or riches
Can ever compare
To the great I am

For I will crush your gods
Of stone, your images, your indifference
To be crushed as if they never were
Says God
And you are left only
With Me, your God, your only God
Who made you
I Am who I Am
In Me are riches of
Which you've never
Dreamed of
That blind eyes can see
You can feel and hear My voice
That calls you in the
Darkness of your soul
And lifts you out
Of what you have created

For naught
I am the water that
Quenches your thirst
As no one can lift you out of
Darkness, to light up your life
And give you peace
Oh, man of indifference
I am your God and Father
And in being your God
You will believe in Me
Or be without Me and be lost
In your unbelief
I will crush your gods into dust
Never to be in My presence
Says the Lord
God Almighty

Being with You

Jesus in my dreams
Sometimes You talk, I remain silent
I just love being with You
Just enjoy being with You
While the enemy looks on

I am with You
And I feel safe
Just enjoying what
You have made and having a
Quiet time with You
Sometimes You ask me
"What do you want Me
To do for you"
But for some reason
I am unable to speak

I am just happy
To be in Your presence
And nothing is more
Important than
Being with You

I feel so safe and
Loved as if nothing
In the world matters
Not at all

The Wonder of You

O God
When You blew the kiss of life
Upon the earth
The heavens opened
And the whole of heaven
Exalted You
In awesome praise
Of your splendor, Your perfection
Of the miracle of life
Seeing its first light
The whole earth shook
With the sacredness
Of your smile You blessed the earth
With the wonder of Your love
That is You, my God

The angels burst forth
In praise and joyous song
And exaltation of time
The whole of heaven
Exalted in joy and love
Of You, holy is the Lord
To the one who is
The King of all now and forever
For You alone
Are holy, holy, holy is the Lord
Heaven and earth
Can pass away
But You, O God, You

Are forever
Your sacredness and perfection
Will be forever
And ever amen

Jesus, I Believe in You

Jesus, I heard Your name
So many times before
It didn't mean too much to me
But that was yesterday long ago
Before I came to know
You personally; I was young and unknowing
I loved You very much but
I saw You as a Judge with
God Almighty; I just didn't think of You too much
I knew You loved me
But that was a distant thought
A distant memory You were there but not in my memory
In my life that much
I feared what You would do
If I were lost, I just didn't
Think I was good enough
To be loved by You; I didn't—know
Doesn't everyone feel that way
And distance
Controlled me then
And indifference too
But now I know You as
My God and personal Savior

I know You now of Your sacrifice
The kind that lays down
His life for his fellow men
I didn't think of You that often
Now I want You

In my mind, in my spirit, in my life
Back then I was just living
Now as I've come to know You better
You are more real—You listen
I learned along the way
That You really care for me
In what I say and what I do
In what I think, the way I think
I live my life now, I see I make time
For You—to pray, to love You, to experience You
Sitting by my side I feel
Your nearness in my dreams
Now I can tell You anything
Of misery, of love, and pain
And in between, but that is in my daily life
All that my heart feels
And my eyes have seen
In my dreams of You, I don't speak
Just enough for You to be by my
Side and have You speak to me in
My dreams in my life

Now I can tell You of
My problems, my pain, my Joy
The injustice, my inspirations
In my life I've grown, I guess I can say
Oh, how lucky can I be
To have You to love me
To defend me, to direct
My life, now my life is full
Because of You; I treasure You
Since I came to know You

You were always there
I was too blind to see to know
Too busy with life; Your love for me now
Is life; things have changed now
I know where I am going
And where I am
And where I'm going to be
Because of You
But now it is more real
I also will make time for
My friend Jesus; I was busy living
And young, too busy and unknowing
Now it's different in how I live
My life now; I choose to be with You
I shall try to live try to be
The person You want me to be
To live up to Your
Friendship, to Your love
For me, my Savior
My love, my God
I may fail now and then
I know You will pick me up
And be by my side
All I can do is try
Imperfect as I am
I know You will accept
Me, my God and Savior
Jesus Christ

God

You have an intricate
And loving nature
Full of promise, full of love

Who can fathom You
Who can try or want to
Enough to know You are
All-loving and good
All-knowing

As a Father, you love us
You protect us
You provide for us
You know our individual needs
You know what we are
To be and can be in You

You are all knowledge
All-encompassing
Our minds cannot
Comprehend the intricateness
Of You, for You are all
Knowing of who we are, who we
Will be, and where we will land

Your knowledge is unfathomable
You know all the world
And other worlds
We know nothing about
You made everything and everyone

And nothing has been made
Or known that you didn't
Know beforehand
You are all in one

You are limitless
And we live in a world of limits
We know as much as You
Want us to know

When we try to go out-of-bounds
We know what happened
To the one who tried
And was found wanting

Enough to know that You are
God—I am who I am
And foolish is the man or angel
Who tries to test Your
Boundaries or limits

He got sent to the pits
Of hell; he still doesn't get it
Quite different of what he wanted
Never to leave but suffer
And all followers and haters
Go there
The opposite of God's world
Which is love, goodness of
Our Father God the Almighty
For all eternity

Gifts of Mother Nature

Mother Nature spreads
Her harvest beauty
Saying here I am
Full of brilliant colors
To spread across
The land
Reds, yellow, and oranges
And all the colors in between
Full of life
Joining with the
Dancing clouds
And magnificent blue sky
To give you a panorama
Of delight
In all its glory
Of fall colors
Before going into
Winter wonderland

The beautiful trees
Spread with gold and reds
Only Mother Nature
Can provide
In the beautiful
Paradise of hills and valleys
Mountains
Glorious to behold
To treasure all your life

Your Joy of Creation, God

Your joy of creation God
Set Mother Nature to singing
At Mother Nature's beauty and song
Being itself excellence of
Earth and heaven
Showed its delight
At Mother Nature being itself
As you started singing
A melodious voice
A Mother Nature show of beauty
With delight, the earth trembled with joy
As the whole of heaven and
Earth worshipped You at
The works of Your hands
And the beauty of Your love
While the animals frolicked
To and fro
Excited at who they were
Loving life

Created from Your loving
Hands and Spirit
Holy God, splendid God

You created song and music
The earth and heaven
To give You glory, to give You joy
The raindrops beat a sweet
Refrain to Your sweet

Melodious voice that set every
Heart to love and worship You
You laughed at the joy
Of Your creation as it rang throughout
You loved the works of Your hands and Spirit
At seeing men go
About their daily life
You saw it was good
Very very good

You loved what You
Had created
Perfect in all ways
And You laughed a joyous
Wonderful laugh
That encircled the
Whole earth with Your love
Thunderous and great
The mountains, rivers
And streams joined in
A joyous crescendo
As the whole earth and heaven
Trembled with joy at being
The trees swaying in the
Breeze, the clouds passing by joined in
The flowers in joyous
Dance at being praising You
While the sun shone its light on all the world
As Your rainbow of Your promise
Overlooking all the earth
Set all the angels to song

The heavens in joyous
Excitement joined in to see

The perfection
You had made in
Every detail
A sight to behold—beautiful
Your wonderful
Thunderous laugh overshadowed all with
Joy at seeing
The earth alive
In all its glory
Your blessings covered
The whole earth
In wonder of being

And men kneeling down
Giving thanks to
The one above who created him

For great was the sight
To behold perfect in all its ways
The creation
Of God Almighty

You saw how good it was
And Your laughter
And joy covered the earth
While You danced in great exuberance
While the angels sang in the heavens
To Your great glory and
Perfection, amen and amen

When You looked upon the
World and saw the perfect
Creations You had made
You marveled at its perfection
Your smile filled
The whole earth
You saw how good it was
The beauty of its trees
The abundance of fruit
And flowers aglow
The mountains with snowy
Peaks and sunny meadows
The birds flying around
In joyous song and energy
In fields of grains of glory
Your streams of water
And rivers started flowing
With exuberance and song

At Mother Nature being itself
Earth and heaven showed its
Delight; You started singing with
Melodious voice as the whole
Of nature shone with delight
And heaven and earth worshipped
You the great I Am Creator
At the works of Your hands
Perfect and wonderful
Are You, the world came into being
As perfection came into being from
Our Creator God Almighty

The Touch of God

The touch of God
No man can comprehend
The intensity
The life force evolving
Moment by moment

By a will, a thought
Of God Almighty

Life in all its glory
The gift is priceless
Worthy to treasure it
Or disbelieve its Maker

And become forever
A question
Forever missing the mark to
What is obvious
To those whose
Sight is through the Spirit

Be a man of belief
And rise to glory with Him
Who breathed the spirit
Of life into the human body
Fashioned with precision
Knowledge and love
All intertwined from
The essence of God

Of the heart of God
A loving Spirit

Holy Spirit God
You sit in stillness
Giving joy to its Maker
And to the world that
Sees Your beauty
Your excellence in
All things in all persons
Great and small

I Am Listening

I have heard you calling in the night
Heard you crying for the light
To make things right
In your life
Come, My child, see the light
God is calling you
With a heart full of love so true
Listen
Come and lay your
Problems at My feet
And let Me enfold you
In My arms
I can help you through
The night; I will still
The fears in your heart
Till the sunshine falls
Down on you
Let Me help you with
The burdens that you carry

Let Me carry all your worries
I'm the one to see
You through the rough
Parts and good parts
In your life
But don't forget Me
In your happy times
All I want to hear
You say is

That you love Me
That you need Me
That you can't live without Me
God is here listening to you
God is here loving you
For all the days of your life
And those to come
In eternity

Make a Joyful Sound
Easter Sunday '92

Praise the Lord
All the earth
Praise Jesus
All of heaven above
All you creatures
Great and small
Praise the Lord above
All you green plants
Flowers and trees
Praise the Lord who
Made you be
All you mountains
Fields and streams
Make the sounds of
Joyful life. Sing to the one
Who gave you life from above
All you waters, sky, and
Sea; fill the earth with purity
All the lights in heaven
Above make a joyful
Song unto the Lord

All the earth
Rocks and trees
Praise the Lord with me

All you people
Praise God our Father

God of unity, God of love
Let the earth
And heavens above
Sing to You all day long
A new song of love
From all humanity sing
In unity
To our Lord God above

Reach Out to Me

You think that I don't
Know that I don't feel
The pain, the tragedies
You suffer on this earth
I cry with you
And in your joys
I laugh with you
I am your God
Your Father
Reach out to Me
I'll be with you to
Shelter you from the storm
I'll be there to cover you
And shelter you from all
Your fears
Says God our Father
Our Jesus God
I'll share in your joys, your songs
Your prayers, your praises
To Me
And when the times are hard
I'll put out My hand to
Cover you with love and protection
Till harm pass by
"I love you," says the Lord Jesus God
"Because you are Mine. I love you"

To Be in Me

My earth is angry at
The ills you have created
And the mountains will roar
And the fires overcome
And destroy
the grounds shake
to wake you up
Why do you not care what you do
What you say; why you don't love Me
Surely you love the earth
This is your home
Until I call you
To be or not to be in Me
For I have always loved you
Even as you turn away
From Me, says Jesus God

Quiet Time with God

The stillness of God
His serenity of His love
When you anticipate His
Wondrous creation
Sitting on top of a mountain
In a quiet gentle stream
In the stillness of the day
You feel His presence
As He sits beside you
In a quiet time
Enjoying His creation
Magnificent, beautiful
And wondrous joyful thoughts
He smiles
And the glorious sun
Smiles down to shine
With rays of gold
To warm your body
Your soul
Your earth
How wonderful it is
To be in God's creation
With Him sitting by
Your side in loving times
And pondering His creation

Prayers to God

Prayers are like
Flowers of God
Blessings of love
Raining down
From above
For those who believe
Streams of living water
Running over you
And to all who believe

Sunlight streaming down
Warming the earth
And all inhabitants

Seeping down into your brain
Into your very soul
Bringing happiness and peace
Being happy and at peace
Enjoying life in God's creation
A happiness that you are alive
In all earth's beauty
And magnificence

You Are Wonderful, Lord

Praise the Lord
Oh, my soul
You are wonderful
You are beautiful
Lord God Almighty

You are the cry
Of my heart
The joy of my soul

In You I find peace
Love and kindness

In You I find life
The joy of tomorrow
And the answer to my
Daydreams in You
As
Nature sings
And the songs of the winds
Embrace the earth
In gladness and joy
The waters cry out
In joyful, dancing
Singing You praises
With exuberance
And praise

While the sun
Shines in all its glory
Only to please You
And together
They cry out in praise to You
With all of nature
To You, God, be the glory
Praising Your name
And all that You are
Full of grace we give You
Praise, love, and thanksgiving
For existence for life

Your Love for Us

In You I rejoice
With all of nature

Thank You for the clouds
As the stars
The fireworks of the
Stars and thunder
Thank You for all
Of nature
All the earth calls You Blessed
Thank You for the rainbow
Your promise to us
You always remember
And never forget
You fill us with your
Love; you love us in each new
Day each and every day
You demonstrate
Your love and joy in us
Our Father
Thank You, God

Thank You, God, I Love You

Thank You, God, for the
Sun, the moon, the earth
The sky
Thank You for
The waters that You
Hold so deep in the earth
In the upper heavens
Only You can know
And us to dream
Of the blending
Of the earth and sky
Of the treasures
In the far beyond
That You hold
In the palms of Your hands
Reserved for those
Abiding in Your love
Our home
For all eternity

Like I Love You

I'm enjoying
The sun shining
On my face—on me
As I lie on the couch I repose
Like the flowers
In early spring's chill
That comes in
And burns our leaves
And the snow covers us
But we awaken again
To a brand-new day
A day of promise
A new embrace
When it is warm
And we start growing again
When the sun's rays fall on us
To warm us to
A new day, a new season, a new
Growth and beauty
Seasons come and seasons go
As a ray of light
But Your love stays
To warm my heart and neuter it
In God's creation
Called life

1983
This Man Called Jesus

There's a man I heard about
Walking around the countryside
He calls Himself Jesus
A lonely soul like me

I hear He has something
That other men have not
He can read all your thoughts
And loves you just the way you are
I've heard

He says He is the Shepherd
Of all the lost and found
He is getting them together
To be His followers
For His final paradise
This man's called Jesus

I wonder if this man
I hear so much about
Is He for real
Is He a God, is He the God
Is He what I'm looking for
Has He found me
I have to know

His promises of glory
His love for fellow men

I wonder if He is talking to me
I wonder if I can—listen
Will listen to this man
Called Jesus

This man has gotten to me
Can't put Him out of my mind
Maybe He's found and is
What I am looking for
But cannot name
This man called Jesus

I want to be His friend
This Jesus
He wants us to be His friend
My God, my Savior
Really—He does
I have to go find Him
And tell Him I'm looking
For Him too, this Jesus
I know I will love You, Jesus

Many New Faces of Love

Your love, O God
Is like rain
Like dewdrops
Falling down from heaven
And saturating us with
Your love

Where the sun, the moon
The air we breath
The gentle wind
Beats out its rhythmic
Movements as if in unison
Saying
I love you, I love you, I love you
I love you
To praise and honor and glorify
Your name, O God, I love You
Throughout the universe
Love enters with
Many new faces
All enveloped in Your love

I Feel Content in Your Love

How You still my heart
O God, when You bless me
When I cry, O God, to You
You give me peace
Your arms
Envelope me
And I feel content
In all Your goodness, in all Your love
I thank You
For being You
And helping me
To be a better me

Great and Merciful Are You

Dear God, my Father
Thank You for Your love
Your goodness
Your great mercy
For Your great understanding

Thank You for the sun
The moon, the stars
That shine so brilliantly
Thank You for the
Milky Way and Your guiding star
I enjoy so much
For the stars the planets
I thank You for the waters
The rivers, the streams
The raindrops, the dewdrops
That kiss my skin with
Your love

You are great, God my Father
In You I trust
In You I live

Praise Be to You,
God Almighty

The song within my heart
Sees all in nature
I call Your name
We are all one in you
Praise Your glorious name
Where there are two
There You are in us
With us

Thank You for Your love
For all that I am
And for all that
I can do in You

Thank You, Lord God
For heaven and earth
That is and is to come
Amen

Praises Be to You, Almighty God and Father

God, You are
Never far away
I look and see You there
In Your creation
I turn and You are there
You are ever-present
Only a prayer away
For Your abiding love, I thank You
Thank You for shining Your love on us
Covering me with
Your grace, Your protection

I am the apple of Your eye
The soul that cries for You
The heartbeat that beats
So strong in Your love

For I can see
You are everything to me
The food of my heart, my soul
Your love is Your gift to us
I am all one in You

You Are the Only God, My Father

Some say we are
Little gods
Here on earth
And hearing that
Troubles me to be
Compared to God Almighty
Is unthinkable in my mind

Yes, we are made in God's image
But we are not gods
In any way
There is only one God
God Almighty
With three persons in
One God
God the Father, God the
Son, and God the Holy Spirit
He cares for His children
So for me I'll remain
A little person
With God the Father
Close to me
It is all I need

All I want is
To be in His loving care
He is a refuge unto me

To be with Him is
Everything
My heart desires

Titles don't mean anything
In God's presence
We are His and
That is enough for me

To be in His presence
In His loving care
In His loving hands
Is all that matters
To me

Do Not Destroy My Earth and Yours

The land cried
Seeing itself denuded
Of vegetation
Crying for the beautiful
Trees that graced its breast
Longing for the shadows
From the trees; the clouds that
Passed by to shade the places
As it cast upon it shadows as
The playful breeze swirled
And cooled its brow
For a while
And the beautiful grasses
And flowers that
Covered it like a cloak
Gave a sign of relief from the sun
A warm welcome cover
Of life from the clouds
Where the creatures great
And small that lived and
Fed upon My bounty
Where is My fertile soil that
Grew in and upon Me

My heart cries to see
My earth, my breast sunbaked and parched
And I turn to see

The waters carrying off
My fertile earth—My soul
Gone and burnt to the ground
I know you have to live
Upon Me and of Me
But do you have to destroy
My very heart, My very soul
Gone and burnt to the ground
But do you have to destroy
My very heart, My very soul
And leave Me naked
To the sun
Never more to savor
In My forest, My beauty
My lovely trees
My vegetation, My very life
I made for you
Where are My hills
My bounty is defiled
My mountains denuded
But short will be the time
When you will miss My
Beauty, My bounty, says the Lord God

Do You Care

My earth, My creation

You go around and pollute
And destroy My earth
The earth I made
For you to enjoy
To plant to reap
You kill My fish
My birds, My animals
My vegetation, My creatures, My creations
My streams, My waters
And pollute My air

You have to live in it too
And you care not
What you do
Yes, I am speaking
To everyone
Do you care how I hurt
You care not
How you hurt Me
For it is My creation
That you want to destroy
Says God

All for what
For personal gain
For power over others
For money, for fame

If only you worked
As hard to not pollute
To clean
To filter out the ills
Of your progress
The ills of your heart
The earth I made for you
The gifts. I made for you

You treat it so lightly
You will live in its
Result
And you'll wonder and
Say, "Did I do this?"
Let My people live; they deserve
To live too; you are killing
My heart, My soul, My
Very life and yours too
Wake up

Destroyers of My earth
My heart cries
You are killing
My people, My joy, My song
Stop before
It is too late
Care for one another
Put your energies
To restoring
To caring, to love
Like some do, but not enough of you
Let nature sing again

Let the waters
Flow again
Let life begin again
My earth, My creation, My people
Or the ills you
Created will
Overshadow you
And you are no more
And you will cry
As I do
When—you have
Ransacked My forests
My earth of your future
And mine
When the very sun will
Cast down its hot breath
Upon you
But you have no forests
No water, no shade
To cool your brow
To shadow your breast
For you have
Destroyed it all
With the trash in the oceans, on the lands
If you keep on your
Path of destruction
Stop while you can
Where you have
Ruined My earth
Polluted the land
And ruin now covers
My face when once

The breeze played
Upon My trees, My hills
And growth blessed My
Land and bounty abounded
Now My heart cries
And do you care
My animals die
And you care not
Turn around and clean
Your earth you live in
On it you will die if
You don't care
From the destruction you
Have caused
Clean it up if you can
While you can
Before it is too late
And you are left with
Nothing but hate
Destruction and uncaring
Alone and sad you
Will be with your
Uncaring heart

Your Love, My Sweet Love

When you walk by
And are near me
I love Your touch, Your presence
Stirring the air with a
Sweet perfume
Like no other
Sweet love
It sets off on a
Journey of discovery
Of true love
For I always
Want You by my side
And I don't want to lose You
I love You, God, sweet love
I feel Your presence
Your protection, Your touch
And sometimes I don't know
You are there; I turn around
And yes, You are
My protection in all things
In all situations
I just want to let You know
How great You are, how much
I love You for the wonder
That is You, my God

Glory Is Fullness to God

Glory is fullness
Of the Spirit
To be in Your loving hands
Is to feel the love as Your voice
Falls as a sprinkling
Waterfall
As it falls and flows as a touch
Of a feather caressing, bubbling
To the ground
Your voice is a strong embrace
A caress full of love
As it filters through
The valleys and the
Mountains
Caressing every tree
Every flower, everything
You have made
Your presence is
A rich perfume
Intoxicating full of love
That fills me with
Your love, Your peace and joy
I never want to leave You
For my heart would
Die within me, my God

Thank You, Lord

Praise You, Lord God Almighty
King of heaven and earth
We give thanks to Your
Glory and Your wondrous
Blessings over the earth

Thank You for the sunshine
That warms my heart anew
Thank You for Your love
That heals my heart and soul too

Thank You, Lord, for all creation
Near and far for people
And animals, land and sea
Renewal of plants
And blessings from above

Thank You for Your perfection
Thank You, Lord, for You
You are the wonder
In my heart and soul
That makes all things new
You set my heart to singing

Singing for You, my Lord
Thank You, Lord
Thank You, Lord God
I praise Your holy name
I praise You in Your glory

In all Your works and wonders
Thank You, Lord God, for
Our strength; You are great
Thank You, You are bigger than life
For the wonder
And perfection
That is You, no man can hold
I thank You
Thank You for my family
That I love so much
For all their gifts
I thank You
For their beauty
Of soul and spirit
For their love and spirit
I thank You
And for their love
Of You that brings
Me joy

God, I Love You

How the birds and animals
Love to play in Your streams
Their happiness knows no bounds
As they frolic to and fro

The clouds fly in a rush
To embrace You, Lord God
To cushion Your feet
To be Your armchair and lounge
To be a comfort to You
The sun loves to play in
Your hair, O God
And the soft breeze
Caresses Your face
Perfection You have
Made for Your glory

The sun shines on You
To sparkle in Your hair
To outshine the brightest
Star to please You
For Your smile is precious
To the earth for the blessings
You have bestowed on her
For Your beauty and Your love
Knows no bounds, God my Father

Song of Music

The song of music
Was born to the
Sound of rolling thunder
Rushing water and tide
Caressing the seashore
With waves of rolling thunder and
Water droplets sparkling in the sun
Raindrops beating
In refrain, the song of music
As if to say here
We are a part of
This marvelous
Creation called God
Of the universe

Winter

And winter
The coolness of your snow
And ice that
Freezes on the earth
Creating new masterpieces
To delight and new worlds to explore
It gives new life
To new beginnings
The whispering winds
The blowing snow
Has many secrets to bestow

The majestic mountains
Let the winds play with their
Snow-covered peaks and the
Breezes caress the hills and valleys
In their season
Visions of delight
In their seasons of time
Dressed in all their
Wonder and golden splendor
Blessings for all
The smile of God is
Upon the earth
For a job well-done
In all its perfect creation

Fall Is Falling into Winter

Fall is falling into winter
Of never-ending delight
Of Your great abundance
And gifts of Your generous
Nature we give You thanks
God, for sunshine skies
And days gone and days to come
Of blessings of
Your brilliance of shining
Light and golden splendor
To appreciate to see and enjoy
Fall, Your wonderful colors
Are warm and beautiful days
My God
The browns, yellows, and
Oranges and colors
In between that only
You can make the masterpieces
That warm the heart
With joy and thanksgiving
A blessing of brilliance and perfection
The birds fly in formation
To a new joy, a new experience
In utter delight, they fly their songs
Ringing out through the sky
All over

Fall

I love fall
The beautiful leaves
Arrayed in
Their fall colors

Swaying in the breeze
And softly falling
In their swaying song

In their last
Hurrah to God

To be used
As living matter
For other life
How great and
Wonderful You are
My God, with Your blessings

Spring Is Springing

Spring
How I love You, God
For this season
Snow melting
Birds chirping
Flowers opening
Their brave faces
To the kiss of the sun

The sun smiling down
With joy and song
To the beginning
Of spring with song
With song singing in the air
As it goes to kiss
Each flower and
Tree—with love

And the breezes blow
Whispering their words
Of love
And gently caressing
The face of spring

Holy Are You, O God

O Lord God my Father
I praise You
I worship You
I adore You, I love You

O great God my Father
You are wonderful, Holy One
Beautiful, glorious
You are merciful
Loving, gentle, and kind

The beauty that is You
Is in us
You created us
For Your joy
To praise You, to love You
To glorify Your name

In heaven and on earth
The whole of humankind
Praises You
Exalts You
To the very
Ends of the beautiful universe

Lady of the Gardens

Lady of the gardens
Mother of all
Oh, lady, as you wander through the
Garden and make a stop at every
Flower that radiates for you
You gather their most sweet perfume
To stay with you when the days are
Dark to gather their sweetness and
Beauty to soften your heart and dry the
Tears from your face and heart
You reach out your arms to
Embrace us like rose petals reaching
For the sun
That tender touch you give
You blow us that kiss of sweetness
The breeze comes alive and
You give us that smile so divine
As the breeze and soft winds whisper
Through the lovely flowers
Whispering "I love you"; the trees
Caressing their beauty and
Strengthening their stay
In the hot hours of the noonday sun
And how they prosper
With your gentle care
Like us, your loving ones
We grow and shine under your loving
And gentle care
We have rain and dewdrops

From the sky, you
Water our gardens in our
Hearts and souls
With your showers of love and
Radiant beauty and divine spirit
With your love and gentle
Probing that we may grow into
A beautiful garden of souls
For God the Father
Creator of all

Jewel of Heaven

Jewel of heaven
Virgin Mother dear
Splendid in your finery
In the colors of the rainbow
The stars pale in your beauty
And the sun dances to be near you
The clouds caress your face
And rejoice to be so chosen
While the breeze plays with
Your lovely hair
The raindrops fall as jewels on you
And sparkle with the light of heaven
Oh, to be so near to you
My heart would leap with joy
Your serenity and gentleness
Bring peace to all who know you
Your smile is like sunshine
Bursting through a cloudy day
Your love is like a million
Caresses to all a-seeking

Heart and soul
Your touch is love; the touch
Of heaven here below

For we who love you
Wait longing for your
Beautiful continence
The wait is long—but short

The dream of arms
Enfolding us in a mother's love
Till softly your caressing
Touch is heaven as you
Pick us up and enfold
Us in your loving arms

9-18
Virgin Mother, Queen of Peace

Virgin Mother, queen of peace
Full of love for one of these
Little children calling you
You come calling with the dawn
Calling all to live for peace
By making changes in our life
Call all to sacrifice
For the world that is one
Holding peace for everyone
Making your decision known
Is to be one of her own
Time of trouble, time of peace
Let your love never cease
She is calling all the roses
To be made a masterpiece of love
As a gift to God above
She needs all colors
Bright and strong
For the Lord, she is calling
Everyone
To come to God above
With the fullness of your love
Doesn't matter where
You've been

Or how long you've
Been away from Him
Your commitment

Full and sincere
Is all that matters
To Jesus God
To cast you in a loving light
That's why He made the
Ultimate sacrifice
For you and me

Mother dear calls us
To be one, one with
Jesus, one with God

God's Only Son

Holy Virgin
Hear my plea from a sinner
Such as me
You who loved your only son
All the heavens cry as one
To the God who made it known
That His only Son was born
To die a death for men alone
No one can understand
Why He died a death
So all alone for men who
Didn't care, who denies Him still
More than once or twice
On the cross to Calvary
He came to set all
Sinners free
A love so true, so strong
So pure
He bore the nails, the scars
So deep that pierced His heart
So deep

His blood did run down
His body full of pain

He felt the nails
Tearing through His flesh
For sinners who deny Him
Still—but Jesus wanted to give

His life to gain eternity
For us in heaven for you and me
Only He could stand
The pain so deep, so hurtful
And strong beyond compare
For us sinners

Yet He gave His love, His life
For you and me
On the road to Calvary
And the pain of unbelief
Tore through flesh
And pure heart so deep
Of sinners' unbelief
On the cross He stood alone
He was nailed to suffer for us
It made God cry; He felt the pain
Of His only Son who suffered—so
Whose life was given
For everyone
Yes, He died and now
He lives
And God smiles from
Above for victory
Earned the test of time
To set all captives
Free
To be renewed in His
Son Jesus Christ
For all eternity

Call to Love

The Virgin Mary is
Calling us to be with
God above
To let the love in our
Hearts be true
And express that joy
And love with you
Don't let the love that's
In your heart
Be torn apart by the
Winds of discontent
For tomorrow you
Will repent
Don't let it be
Too late for you

Love of God's Only Son
Easter Sunday 1992

Dear Mary Mother of God
How your heart did break
To see your son carrying
The cross on the way
To Calvary
Your heart breaking in two
To see Him suffering
Giving His life for His
Fellow men
Did they care while
They gambled for
His cloak—no
Only later would they
See the price being paid
For them for us
Oh, sweet Jesus
Thank You for Your pain
For the cross
For Your precious
Blood for sinners
Such as we

Teach Us to Love

Virgin Mary, song of love
Radiant splendor from above
You came to fill our hearts
With love
With the gift of your newborn son
You came to fill all
Hearts with love and joy
To pray unceasingly to God above
To unite all children
Is your heart's desire
To praise God to do His will
On earth
Teach us to pray the
Way you do
Teach us to love the
Way you do
Teach us to love
What you hold true
The time is near
For your only son
To come live on the earth
And be as one with us
With love for all

What Action Did You Take?

Dear Mary
Mother of God
How your heart did break
To see your only son
Carrying the cross
For all humanity

Your heart did break in two
To see Him suffering so
With the cross
On His shoulders with our sins
Being beaten down
With blows so painful
And words unkindly said
To hurt, to pierce
A tender, loving heart
Through flesh, through
Bone to every part of Him
That made His blood
Pour forth for all
Humanity with love and tender
Spirit; how big a price to pay for you and me

Did you see yourself
Standing there
Being hateful
As can be
To a life so pure
Beating just for you and me

Did you pick up that
Stone to let it fly
Not caring what you did
With words and insults
To find its mark
On a heart so true, so pure
Do you feel the shame
Of your actions
Do you still disbelieve
For the God who died for you
Or do you repent
And ask forgiveness
From Jesus God who suffered for you
Fall on your knees and
Ask forgiveness
Before it is too late

Queen of Heaven

Beautiful Virgin Mary
Beautiful as the Christ Child
Fortress of hope and
Inspiration
Lover of peace and beauty
Of heart and soul
Come shine your loving light on us
And let us be a joy to you
And seeing your love for us
Will inspire us to
Love others
As you love us
Beautiful Virgin Mother
With your arms open
Wide to enfold us

We come to you, O Virgin Mary
Mother of the universe
Give us peace and comfort
In our hearts and in our world

Help us to join hands
In a loving circle
Of love
That will transform
The world in peace

Keep us safe
From the storms
Of change

Let your beautiful countenance
Be like sunshine on
A cloudy day
Full of rays of
Hope, love, and peace

That everyone who
Sees your beauty and love
Be moved and inspired
By your grace, serenity
And love
Acknowledging that
You truly are

The Queen of Peace
The Queen of the Cosmos
Together with Christ we can
make a change in our fellow men
a difference in the world
through prayer and love
For all of eternity

About the Author

Writing is something I like to do, to bring to life words and thoughts, bring joy and love to people. It so happened that a book was in the making in praise to Lord God and His creation together with Father God and Holy Spirit.

I'm a mother and enjoy mother nature and all its beauty.